THE MUSIC OF GOD

THE MUSIC OF GOD

Parables of Life and Faith

Segundo Galilea

MEYER
STONE
BOOKS

Translated by John Eagleson

"The Parable of the Dissatisfied People" was first published as "Between India & New York" in *Commonweal,* February 8, 1985, pp. 82–83.

Original Spanish edition: *La música de Dios,* Paulinos, Bogotá, 1987.

Published in the United States by Meyer-Stone Books, a division of Meyer, Stone, and Company, Inc., 714 South Humphrey, Oak Park, IL 60304

Cover design: Ron Henz, R H Studio

Manufactured in the United States of America
92 91 90 89 88   5 4 3 2 1

Library of Congress Cataloging in Publication Data

Galilea, Segundo.
    The music of God.

    Translation of: La música de Dios.
    1. Parables   2. Meditations.   I. Title.
BX2186.G3213   1988   242   87-62873
ISBN 0-940989-20-4

Contents

Preface

In this book I have tried to approach certain questions about the human condition through the form of parables. Some of the questions are of perduring importance, others are particular to our times, and some are of particular concern to Christians.

When using a parable style, we do not treat the topics thoroughly and completely, nor do we follow a systematic order of presentation. The purpose of a parable is not to elaborate a doctrine, but rather to communicate symbolically a simple and essential message. Parables do not speak so much to the logical mind as to the heart. This is why parables were the style preferred by Jesus, by the biblical authors, and by the spiritual wisdom of the Christian and non-Christian East.

As is the case with all parables, the reader will find meanings and applications beyond those suggested by the author. For this reason the book might be useful for group reading or discussion.

The origin of these parables is not important. Some come out of my own experience, some from my imagination, and some are borrowed from the wisdom of the East.

— 1 —

The Music of God

Love is revealed in words.
When words are not enough,
it is revealed in deeds.
When deeds are not enough,
love resorts to music.
Creation is the music of God.
                    —*Indian proverb*

——— Θ ———

The love of God is revealed in a human way: through
God's Word, through the deeds of God's providence, and
through God's music.

We can hear the music of God in nature. We can listen
to God in the murmuring of the sea or in the silence of the
sky and the mountains. At those moments we become part
of a music that leads us to its Author.

But when we hear the noise of traffic or factories, or the
whine of sirens or computers, or the wonders of modern
technology, it might not seem to be the music of God.

It can be difficult to perceive the Musician when the Musician has handed over the score to human beings and has left it to their initiative and creativity to fashion the instruments and the melodies.

Let us learn to listen to God in the music of every invention and in the rhythm of human progress. Let us learn to behold in these scores as well the Composer of all music.

The Middle God

— 2 —

The Parable of
the Accommodating Angel

Two men asked an angel to allow them to share in the power of God. The angel agreed.

The first man asked to be able to do extraordinary deeds. The angel said to him: "You will have the power to do only wondrous deeds. But you will have no special power for ordinary things."

Amazed, the man began to perform wondrous deeds: he read people's minds, he made large sums of money in business and gambling, he created great inventions. And he was very happy. But it wasn't long before he lost his job, and he could do nothing about it. Then his wife left him, and he couldn't do anything about it. He got so sick he could hardly walk, and he could do nothing about it. And he was happy no longer.

The second man asked to be able to do ordinary things. The angel granted his request and said to him that God would not give him power to do anything extraordinary.

And the man continued his life as before, with his modest job, his family, and his health. And he thanked the angel because the angel had made him happy.

———— Θ ————

When I hear someone thank God only for "miracles" or for seemingly extraordinary graces that they have received, I become very sad. Why should we thank God only for extraordinary things, as if God intervenes on our behalf only when no human hope remains? Why should we think of God and turn to God only in the hope of something marvellous?

Our everyday life should be full of occasions for thanking God. For the wonder of being alive and of staying alive. For being able to love and be loved. For every moment of happiness. For enduring evil without being destroyed. For a strong heart to overcome the misery that surrounds us.

All this would be impossible without the "miracle" of God's intervention in every detail of our daily lives. And often we do not appreciate this miracle until we lose something that we have always had: health, love, moments of happiness, life itself.

The Case of
the Journalist and the Bishop

I read in the local press that the bishop asked for prayers in all the churches for God to send rain. The region had been without rain for too long. That very night the weather report confirmed previous forecasts: it would rain within a few days.

In the middle of the week it rained abundantly, and the following Sunday everyone went to church to thank God for the rain.

The following day, a journalist thought it his duty to comment on this event. He spoke positively of the role of science and criticized the superstitious inconsistency of religion in general and the bishop in particular. "The time is gone," he wrote, "when God and religion can substitute for science. Meteorological analysis tells us whether it will rain or not, and why. To pray for rain is a sign of ignorance and religious fanaticism; this might have been understandable in a pre-scientific world...."

———— Θ ————

It seems to me that the journalist was not as progressive as he thought. At least he is less progressive than the old bishop. For the bishop also heard the weather report, and he knows very well that when it rains it is because of climatic conditions that can be systematically studied by science. He knows that God is not someone who goes around blowing the clouds this way and that to answer people's prayers.

But the bishop knows something that the journalist does not know. He knows that religion is not incompatible with science. Moreover, he knows that both are necessary to understand the totality of reality and events. As for the recent rainfall, he knows that both assertions are true at the same time: it rained for scientific reasons, and it rained because God wanted it to rain. For in every event there are two dimensions: the scientific dimension and the religious dimension, the level of causes as verifiable by science and the level of the ultimate meaning of those causes.

When the weather forecaster reported that it would rain, he was correct: he spoke on the scientific level. But weather forecasting is not theology.

When the bishop asked the people to thank God for the rain, he was also right: the religious level is as real as the scientific, but it is deeper. The bishop believes in science, but he also knows that science is a creation of God and is in God's hands.

In prayer we pass from the scientific level to the religious level of life. Whenever we see the love and the providence of God behind the rain, behind the doctor and the medicine that heals us, behind our friend, our spouse, our joys, and our life itself, we are praying.

This is a good way to learn to pray and to experience God in our everyday lives.

But it is also true that there are realities in which we cannot see God, for they are caused by the sin of human beings: hatred, injustice, vice, misery, corruption....

Then how do we pray? How do we experience God?

I believe that we can also experience God in God's absence. Evil is what happens when God is not there. Then prayer is to ask God to act where God is not present.

— 4 —

Power and Mercy

A woman wanted very much to make others happy. She asked God for a share in divine power. God gave her power, and the woman began to change the lives of others. But neither the woman nor the others achieved happiness.

Then the woman asked God for a share in divine love. God gave her love, and the woman began to love others and to respect them just as they were. And the woman and the others discovered happiness.

——— Θ ———

God has been revealed as all-powerful and all-merciful at the same time. This is the foundation for faith, prayer, and hope.

But this is also the source of doubt. If God is so good and has the power to do anything, why is there so much evil and human misery? This apparent aberration is transformed into a luminous mystery with the coming of Christ, who embodies for us the goodness and the power of God.

8

In Christ we see that the power of God is channeled through love. Toward us, God is first of all love, and God uses power to express love.

Christ taught us that human dignity is to be found in loving. For God, this dignity and the human freedom to love or not to love is what comes first. If God "controlled" human beings though divine power, God would dehumanize us. God would not love us as we are. Evil occurs when human beings abuse this love. This is the price God pays for having loved us and respected us as we are, putting the law of love over the law of power.

The law of love implies freedom, which in turn implies that sin and evil can occur. God loves human beings so much that God bets on us, and then totally respects us. God does not hedge the bet, forcing us with divine power. And God took this risk because Christ, through his life and death, made it possible even for evil to be included in the horizon of love.

The mystery of evil is that it is the shadow, still excluded, of love.

— 5 —

The Parable of
the Two Evils

Two men were traveling in a boat. One was well educated
and the other ignorant. The educated man asked the ignorant one if he knew anything about medicine, and the
ignorant man said no. The educated man said that that
was too bad, because he would lose his health.

Then the educated man asked if the ignorant man knew
anything about politics, and the ignorant man said no.
And the educated man said that that was too bad, because
he would lose his rights.

Then he asked the ignorant man if he knew anything
about law, and the ignorant man said no. And the educated man said that that was too bad, because he would
lose all his lawsuits.

Just then the boat overturned and sank. And the ignorant man asked the educated man if he knew how to
swim. And the educated man said that he did not, because his studies had allowed him no time to learn. And

the ignorant man said that that was too bad, because he would lose his life.

———— Θ ————

Evil surpasses our comprehension because it is relative to the goodness of God, which is absolute. Although every evil dehumanizes — whether hunger, sickness, vice, death — every dehumanization is relative to the only absolute dehumanization, namely, the frustration of the destiny of the human being. Thus for all the religions of the world the worst evil is moral evil, because it leads to the only absolute evil.

In the last analysis we cannot know when a temporal evil is really evil within the total horizon of our life. A particular evil could be a good in relation to absolute goodness. Is an illness very definitely an evil, or could it be an evil that leads to good? Who knows? Is a premature death a definite evil, or could it be good in relation to absolute goodness? Who can say?

The mystery of evil can be better understood if we remember that separation from God is the only absolute evil for human beings.

— 6 —

Vessels of Clay

Faith without crisis is infantile.
Faith always in crisis is adolescent.
Faith beyond crisis is adult.
— *From the Christian mystical tradition*

───── Θ ─────

Crises and the temptation to doubt are part of true faith. Without them faith does not mature; it does not grow. Faith is the ability to overcome doubt and reaffirm belief in the midst of crisis.

There is no need to invent such crises. Life itself provides them: the seeming silence of God, the persistence of evil, the unpopularity of faith, our daily frustrations. It is in these crises that faith is made stronger or is weakened, for we carry it in vessels of clay.

Is this not one of the reasons for the certitude of faith? That identical experiences will increase the faith of some but diminish it for others? That some find God in their crises, and others are estranged from God by the same crises, from the God who is offered to them in the midst of their crises?

Fear and Faith

Little faith can cause fear.
Much faith ends all fear.
Little faith can cause superstition.
Much faith ends all superstition.

— Christian experience

——— Θ ———

The Gospels tell us that one night, while the apostles were in their boat, Jesus approached them walking on the water. They didn't recognize him and became frightened, because they thought he was a ghost. At last they did recognize him and were not so frightened.

And Jesus reprimanded them because they had little faith, and their little faith made them see ghosts where there were no ghosts.

— *8* —

The Parable of
the Two Religions

A young woman who wanted to understand true religion approached a wise man for counsel. The wise man sent her out to interview theologians of various religions.

One theologian explained his religion to the woman, making her see that not everything in his religion could be understood, and that faith was required to accept the mysteries and truths that our intelligence cannot grasp.

The young woman was attracted to this religion, but she was uncomfortable with so much mystery.

Another theologian explained her religion, which was very easy to do, for there were no mysteries and the beliefs were easy to understand. The young woman liked this.

She returned to the wise man and said, "I've found the religion I was looking for. Everything is understandable and there are no mysteries or dogmas of faith."

The wise man answered her: "That very definitely proves that the religion you like so much is not the true religion, but that it was made by human beings to human measure. A religion with mysteries and truths that we do not understand clearly, but that are reasonable, comes from God. God is so different from us, and our intelligence is so limited before God, that we are dazzled when God communicates divine truths to us, and we cannot see. Too much light blinds us. That is why we need faith to receive the Light."

— *9* —

The Case of
the Restless Young Woman

There once was a very restless young woman who was always looking for the best alternatives until she got what she wanted.

She began to study a profession, but this did not satisfy her. She found a better alternative and graduated in another profession better suited to her.

She was engaged to a young man, but he left her. She was undaunted by this and found a better man, and she married him.

At first things went badly in her business and she went bankrupt several times. But each time she began again, pursuing better options, and finally her business prospered.

She became interested in politics and joined a political party. But after awhile she was no longer convinced by the party line, so she changed parties and continued working for her ideals.

She had always been very religious, but as the years passed she found herself further and further away from the church. Religion seemed less important than before, and she finally left it behind. So she looked for a substitute. But the more that she searched and increased her dedication to politics, to her ideas, to her profession, and to her family, she could find no alternative or experience that could replace her lost religion.

And there was a great void in her life, and for once she could not find a substitute.

―――― Θ ――――

Religion is a value that has no substitute or alternative. Other values and ideals can be recovered in analogous experiences, and there are always alternatives to the failures in our lives.

But for lost religion there is no alternative — except to return to it.

The Parable of
the Naïve Mother

A mother had a son she wanted to educate as well as she could and to whom she wished to teach her values.

And so she took great pains to assure that he should learn to speak and to read and to write very well. She chose a fine school for him, where he learned foreign languages, for she knew that these would be useful to him in the future. As she belonged to a family with prestigious ancestry, she taught her child about family traditions and family values. She taught him her moral principles and inculcated into him her very deep-rooted sense of social justice.

The mother was a believer, but she was not a churchgoer. And she decided that in matters of religion it was better not to impose anything on her child, but rather to wait for him to grow up and choose a religion for himself. In this way she would respect his freedom. She did not baptize him, so that he could be baptized later on as a personal option if he so chose. Nor did she send him to Sunday school or teach him the prayers that she knew.

The child grew up and was old enough to choose his own values. He decided upon a career and a commitment to social justice. He chose a wife and established a household based on his family values. But he had no interest in religion. He did not choose the religion of his parents. He had no motivation to be religious, and in the atmosphere where he lived and worked nothing attracted him to the faith. Although he occasionally read about Christianity, the ideas in the books did not reach his heart.

-------- Θ --------

The values of Christian faith are not chosen by a simple rational process or by study. Nor are they decided upon "spontaneously." Faith comes through the word of God that is communicated to us "from outside," through evangelization and through education. Faith is received as a gift, just as a child receives the gift of life without having chosen it.

The mother of the parable was naïve to think that a young person would choose faith without having been motivated to do so and without having first experienced the values of faith.

The mother was inconsistent, because on the one hand she thought — quite rightly — that she was not violating her child's freedom when she educated him from birth in her values: language, schooling, ethical principles. But on the other hand she thought that religion was something different, that it did not need to be part of the child's development, that it should not be "imposed."

Far from being an imposition on the child, it is a duty for parents to give their children the best that they have, including their faith. Just as no one expects that a child should first grow up before deciding what language to learn or whether to go to school or not, so too religious experience should be offered the child as a basic value. For it is not up to the child to choose what is a necessary part of the gift of life.

— 11 —

The Parable of
the Demolished House

Two women lived next door to each other. Both were very religious.

They learned from a reliable source that in the future their houses were to be expropriated and demolished and that the government would offer the owners a place to live in a distant region. Everything would be prepared for them and they would not have to worry about finding housing. They would be responsible only for travel expenses.

The first woman did not believe any of this. Instead she set about expanding and improving her house. She lived on the hope that her house would last forever, and that she would pass it on to her children, and they to their children, for generations to come. She was obsessed with having the best and the sturdiest house possible, and she even improved it by adding modern conveniences. She was always unhappy, for her purchases were never what she expected, and the neighborhood services that she had no control over were quite unsatisfactory. She invested everything she earned in her house. As she was a religious person, she prayed to God every day about the problems and progress of her house.

The second woman believed the news about the expropriation. She kept up her house decently well, but she was not continuously worried about improving it. She was content with her basic necessities and was not frustrated by any lack of creature comforts. Rather, she saved up for the long trip and spent her time learning about the place she would be traveling to and the best route to get there. As she too was religious she prayed to God every day that the problems of her house would not distract her from her concern for a better house and a safe trip.

Many years passed, and one day, unexpectedly, the expropriation and demolition occurred. The first woman was left homeless and did not know where to go. The second happily undertook her journey.

————   Θ   ————

All the religions of the world believe in a divinity. But not all believe in a future life. The sign of a true believer is not only to believe in God, but in a God who offers us everlasting life. What changes our attitude toward life is not so much belief in God, but rather the conviction that our definitive dwelling is not here.

— *12* —

The Parable of
the Severe Winter

Is it inappropriate to speak of eternal life to the poor and suffering?

——— Θ ———

There once was a very poor neighborhood where the winter was very harsh and the people suffered greatly from the cold.

During these winters the people organized as well as they could. They were able to find some firewood, and some of the families helped each other out and shared what they had. But life was very hard for them.

The pastor of the neighborhood church did what he could to help, but there was not much he could do. He tried to encourage the people by reminding them that winter did not last forever and that soon spring would arrive and then summer and that life would be good again. For the mild season in that country was long and kind.

Some began to criticize the pastor saying that to speak to the people about a summer in the future distracted them from their present reality and their struggles to improve it.

And the pastor responded: "The summer that is coming is just as real as winter and all its problems. And when we speak of what is real that is never a distraction, but rather it gives the people hope. The people have the right to include the coming summer in their harsh reality, to include it in their struggles and their efforts, for summer is just as real as winter. Not to speak of summer would indeed be a disservice, for then the people would not be considering their reality as a whole, with the hope that is part of it.

"Moreover, you can see for yourselves that just because the people are waiting for summer does not mean that they stop trying to overcome the problems of winter and make it more bearable and human."

— *13* —

The Parable of
the Sweethearts

A young man was very much in love with his fiancée, and
she was very much in love with him. Their engagement
had already lasted for a long time, and everyone agreed
they were made for each other. They had decided to get
married when he finished his studies.

But then the country went to war, and the young man
had to join the army. He had to leave very quickly before
the wedding, with hardly time to say goodbye to his grief-
stricken sweetheart.

The war lasted a long time, and the young man had
to stay at the front. He had no news from his sweetheart,
for the war prevented communication. But he continued
to be hopelessly in love.

During the difficult days and long nightwatches, the
young man continuously thought about his sweetheart.
And he imagined over and over again his return, how
she would still be waiting for him, just as he so anxiously

waited to see her. He dreamed about the tremendous joy of the reunion, of the wedding, and the profound happiness of their life together.

But as time passed he also began to have doubts and fears and to mistrust his grand hopes. What if she was no longer waiting for him, if her love for him had faded, if she had married someone else? What if their reunion was not the explosion of joy he had dreamed of but rather a disappointment? And the young man began to be afraid of returning home.

Finally peace came and the young man returned to his home. He found his sweetheart and the reunion he had dreamed of for so long occurred. And the young man could not believe how happy he felt, for the reunion surpassed his most optimistic dreams. Her love for him had been always the same as he felt for her, and the reunion was unimaginably joyful. They hoped their happiness would never end.

——— Θ ———

The prophet Isaiah says:

> Like a young man marrying a virgin,
> so will the one who built you wed you,
> and as the bridegroom rejoices in his bride,
> so will your God rejoice in you. [62:5]

Every encounter of two lovers on earth is a symbol and a foretaste of the encounter with God in heaven.

If the encounter of two persons in love causes such joy, what will be the joy of our encounter with God?

If this is what occurs with human beings, with our

fragile and fickle hearts, what must it be like to encounter God, whose heart does not change?

We are willing to endure suffering and waiting to meet the persons we love, although they can never completely fill our hearts and sooner or later will disappoint us. Of how much greater value, then, is the suffering and waiting for the promise of the encounter with the One who is more than our hearts can hold.

— *14* —

The Parable of
the Dirty Logs

A group of young people had started a huge bonfire because it was very cold. To feed the fire they brought logs from the forest.

Much of the wood was dirty, covered with mud and dust, and some of it was wet, so it did not easily catch fire. But, little by little, the fire itself burned through the mud and dust and dried out the wood. And in the midst of sparks and smoke the logs, now clean and purified, ignited and became part of the bonfire.

————— Θ —————

The bonfire is God and the fulness of divine love and happiness. We are the logs.

The destiny of human beings is to participate in the fulness of God, that is, happiness without shadows and love without limits or end.

But very often the human spirit is not clean enough to

be ignited by the fire of perfect communion with God and other persons. Sins, even small sins, defects, blindness, selfishness, continuously muddy our spirits. We are not ready to catch fire in the blaze of the infinite happiness of God. And since God wants us to share in the divine happiness, God helps us to purify our spirits of everything that is incompatible with God.

This purification normally happens during our lives. Human life will always have a dimension of purification that prepares us for the fire of the happiness of God. This is the ultimate meaning of suffering, contradictions, crosses, sickness, misery, and especially of the radical purification that occurs in death. The ideal at the moment of death is for our spirits to be purified and clean so that it can ignite immediately in the blaze of happiness that is never consumed.

But this is not always the case. Human beings do not always take advantage of the possibilities for purification that God offers us during our lives. Or if we do take advantage of them (for often our suffering and the crosses we have to carry purify us in spite of ourselves), we may have accumulated so many impurities that our purification is insufficient. Many die unprepared to enjoy completely the happiness that is their destiny.

It is then that the love of God, determined that we should have no obstacles to our joy, intervenes to complete the purification of our spirit, to prepare us for the inextinguishable love for God and for others.

We do not understand how God purifies us after death. It is a mystery, like everything relative to our passing into eternity. We cannot even imagine what it will be like, for there is nothing on earth that can serve as a point of reference.

Christian tradition calls this purification after death Purgatory. Purgatory is not a punishment. It is not an arbitrary penance imposed by God. Purgatory is the inescapable and beneficial result of the dirty log coming in contact with the fire. Purgatory is the mercy of God who helps us prepare for the blaze of everlasting love and happiness.

It has been said that the purification of Purgatory — as a continuation of the purifications of our life on earth — implies suffering. But, again, this is not because God wants us to suffer. The dirty log becomes part of the fire as the mud and the moisture are burned away in the midst of crackling and smoke. So too the evil to which we have become so attached must be burned away.

— 15 —

The Mystery of Old Age

> There is a time to prepare and a time to produce.
> There is a time to grow and a time to decay.
> There is a time to receive and a time to give.
> There is a time to be born and a time to die.
> There is a time for fulness and a time for purification.
>
> *— Biblical paraphrase*

One of the contradictions of modern society is its obsession with prolonging life, while at the same time it casts aside and abandons its old people. The extremes of human life — infancy and old age — are very similar in their vulnerability and defenselessness, their apparent uselessness, their lack of "logic."

But if God is the source of life, no human life is useless, and a prolonged old age must have value and meaning. It may be impossible to talk about this without taking into consideration the religious dimension of life, and perhaps that is why in very secularized societies the situation of old people is particularly precarious and painful.

In the final analysis, I believe that, like children, old people are a special presence of God, and like children they are closer to God than we are. This is not only because they are closer to death, not only because old age brings wisdom and so for many a return to religion and lost values. (The presence of old people in the churches is a sign of the wisdom of faith.) Their closeness to God is also because the twilight of life is a time of purification.

It is said, and rightly so, that in old age psychological traits and defects are accentuated. But we can also see that many habitual vices and sins of the past are purified and sometimes eliminated. The spirit becomes more humble, perhaps because life no longer has much to offer, and solitude aids the poverty of spirit. There are no longer idols or false illusions and promises to worship. And this makes old people wiser and more contemplative. This is the ultimate conversion, enclosed in external deterioration.

Old age is a form of spirituality, and should be lived on that level. This is what gives meaning to those lives apparently marginalized and finished: a profound purification that prepares us for the vision of God and anticipates the mystery of Purgatory. It is a witness to the fragility of life and our human projects and to the irreversible deterioration of the present life.

Old age is the darkest hour of life. For that reason it is also the vigil of life's definitive dawn.

— *16* —

The Parable of
the Nun and the Orphans

There once was a very holy nun who had a home where she had gathered together various orphans to take care of them. She was very self-sacrificing and gave them everything that they needed. And she was very affectionate toward them, no matter what the defects and ingratitude of the children.

As the children got older, their defects and errors became more apparent, and they did not listen to the nun. But she loved them as much as ever and gave of herself without expecting them to improve their behavior or to treat her in the same way she treated them.

The youngsters began to feel badly about their poor response to this gratuitous love. And life in the home became more and more difficult, for they could not bear for someone to love them just as they were and expect nothing in return. And they started to find ways to improve.

One tried to correct his defects, to become more worthy

of the love that he received. But he was unable to do this. And so he ended up with a guilty complex and no longer could accept the nun's affection.

Another tried to be as good to the nun as she was to him. But he was selfish and was not able to show as much affection as he would have liked. And so he felt worse than ever and was unable to endure the nun's goodness.

Others felt so unworthy of the nun's charity that they left the home to live with people whose friendship was like their own, who treated others well or badly according to their merits. But eventually they found themselves quite alone and friendless, for people looked more at their bad points than their good ones and always expected something in return for their friendship.

Others were resentful and became aggressive toward the nun, because deep down they wanted her to be as selfish as they were. They could not tolerate her gratuitous love and they ended up quite neurotic.

But there were some others who decided to be more humble and to accept being loved unconditionally and just as they were. And this freed them from their complexes and tensions and brought them great peace and self-acceptance. And it helped them love their companions just as they were and to accept each other unconditionally and gratuitously.

------- Θ -------

To accept that God first loved us, through no merits of our own, and that God is always there for us, although we forget God, is more difficult for us than following God's commandments.

To accept that God loves us just as we are, unconditionally, gratuitously, and forever, is more difficult for us than to sacrifice as we should for God and for others.

To accept that God forgives and forgets absolutely and does not hold our past against us is more difficult for us than to repent of the evil we have done.

To accept this love of God is the only path to liberation and interior peace. And it is the underlying reason why we should accept each other and love each other unconditionally and just as we are.

— 17 —

The Parable of
the Jealous Husband

The disciple asked the master how to understand God's love for every human being. For no matter how many people there are, God's love is always personal, special, as if each person were the only one on earth.

And how can it be that persons who know that they are loved by God above all things do not become jealous of each other?

The wise master answered with two comparisons:

There was a young couple who were very much in love. The husband was very jealous, because his wife was very affectionate and loved not only her husband but also other people who were close to her: her daughter, her parents, her brother, and her friends. And her husband was jealous of all of them, for he wanted her to dedicate all her interest and affection to him. And though they loved each other very much, the marriage was very precarious because of his jealousy.

But finally the husband was able to understand that there are different kinds of loves and affections, and that each is unique and special according to the person who is the object of the love. And all of these loves are expressed simultaneously and one love does not hurt another. The love for our parents, the love for our children, the love for our brothers and sisters, the love for our friends does not diminish at all the love for our spouse. Rather it strengthens it.

———— Θ ————

Once there was a young girl who had many very good friends, and they loved each other very much and often visited each other.

And little by little she discovered what genuine friendship means: that each friend was someone special for her and each relationship was unique in its meaning and richness. And the number of her friends did not diminish her affection for each one; rather it increased it. It was as if each friend were the only one in the world.

———— Θ ————

And finally the master said: "These examples are a pale reflection that can help us understand something of the intimacy and the depth of the love of God for every person, regardless of how many human beings there are on earth."

— *18* —

The Symbol of
the Greatest Love

Love one another,
as I have loved you.
A man can have no greater love
than to lay down his life for his friends.
You are my friends, if you do what I command you.
I shall not call you servants any more,...
I call you friends.

— John 15:12–15

In his discourse on love as the essence and fundamental requirement of his message, Jesus chose the love of friendship as the best symbol of what he meant: "You are my friends,...I call you friends...." The greatest love is to sacrifice for your friends.

Love has many forms. The love of friendship, but also the mother's love for her children, the love for our parents, the love of our brothers and sisters, the love of courtship and conjugal love. Jesus could have chosen one of these other forms of love as a symbol of his commandment to love and as its highest expression. And at first glance it seems that he should have, for friendship does not seem to be the most intense expression of human love.

Indeed, maternal love could have been the most appropriate. Or even more the love of sweethearts or spouses, which is the most intense and total expression of love between two human beings.

It is true that the love of friendship does not have the passion, the concentration, and the intensity of the love of a couple. But it is also true that the symbol of friendship chosen by Jesus is the most profound and decisive of all. For in the last analysis, as our experience itself attests, the supreme form of all human love is true friendship.

The love of friendship must be present, sooner or later, in the other forms of love if they are to perdure. The love we have for our family or the love of a couple is precarious and fickle if this love is not also transformed into friendship. And this transformation cannot be presupposed; rather it must be brought about through the arduous path of the love of friendship.

There are parents and children who are not friends. There are brothers and sisters who are not friends. And this makes the family very vulnerable, as we know very well. Likewise there are many couples, spouses, and lovers who do not achieve true friendship. (When lovers are not also friends, if there relationship as a couple ends, everything else often ends as well.)

In all these cases experience teaches us that in the end it is very difficult to free our love from the selfishness or ingratitude that gradually weaken it. Or to keep our love intact once the passion that was present at the beginning begins to lose its power.

Without friendship love cannot resist the trials of suffering or the test of time. For no attraction, infatuation, or passion is permanent. They all suffer the continuous chilling of dissatisfaction and human limitation, of the pain and loneliness present in every human heart, and of the precariousness of every love that is based on passion and feeling.

When conjugal love has crossed the threshold of all the crises of life and the attrition of time, what remains is the affection of deep friendship. This friendship is the will to continue sharing, sacrificing, and giving to each other, beyond the satisfaction of the senses and the heart.

For Jesus there is no greater love than this. That is why he offers it as a symbol of his own love.

— 19 —

The Case of
the Frustrated Woman

A child was growing up, and she learned to eat and to dress herself and to play, and she was quite excellent at sports. But she did not learn to speak her own language. The years passed, and she became an adult, and she still could not speak the language of her people. And although she knew how to do many things, she lived a life of great frustration.

―――― Θ ――――

Prayer is not a luxury for religious persons. Prayer — our personal relationship with the Source of love and life — is a requirement for human beings. We are made for prayer, "programmed" for it, just as we are made to speak our own language. We all have a contemplative core that needs to be developed in prayer. Persons who do not cultivate this core might have many good qualities, but they are dehumanized at a very deep level.

Hunger for God

A man was very busy with his work and his many respon-
sibilities. He was so busy that he hardly had time to eat or
sleep. He earned a lot of money, he became very famous,
he accomplished much — but eventually he died of anemia.

——— Θ ———

If we allow no time to pray in the midst of all our concerns,
it brings anemia and spiritual death. We feel immediately
the effects of physical hunger, and we want to eat, but we
do not feel the effects of spiritual hunger except in the long
run, when it may be too late.

Our physical instincts make us eat, but only the instinct of faith makes us pray. Our first instinct is hunger
for bread; the second is hunger for God. For Jesus said
that we do not live by bread alone but also by the nour-
ishment that satisfies our hunger for God.

Prayer not only satisfies our hunger for God, but also
stimulates and increases it. The human paradox is that

we are dehumanized if we do not satisfy our hunger for God, and we are dehumanized as well if we cease to feel this hunger. The paradox of the life of the Spirit is that to be satisfied we must first feel the desire for God; both are necessary at the same time.

To be hungry for bread is bad, but to be hungry for God is good. To fill ourselves with bread so that we are no longer hungry is good; but it is not good to fill ourselves with God so that we no longer hunger for God. The more our physical hunger increases the more degrading it is, but the more our spiritual hunger increases the more noble we become.

If millions of people in the world suffer hunger for bread, it is because other millions are not hungry for God. For it is impossible to be hungry for God and to try to satisfy that hunger without wishing at the same time to share our bread with those who are hungry.

— *21* —

The Parable of the Daily Meal

We can find God everywhere—in the street, in our work, in others, in events—if these make us think about God. And so the believer can pray often throughout the day.

Why then should we have special times, longer periods, set aside for prayer?

———— Θ ————

There once was a woman who was so busy that she had time to eat only crackers, or at best snacks grabbed at odd moments throughout the day. Eventually she got sick. And she was put on a diet of two meals a day, which she had to digest slowly, and she had to allow time for this.

———— Θ ————

It is not enough to live on snacks on the run, no matter how many snacks we eat, to keep up our strength. We need also to eat something more substantial and nourishing. We need to chew it well and leave time to digest it properly. Our longer periods of prayer are to digest and to deepen, slowly, the brief encounters we have had with God during the day.

— *22* —

The Parable of
the Corrupt City

There once was a city whose inhabitants lived without God and without any moral law. Families had disintegrated and the people were dissolute. The politicians and government leaders were corrupt and were out only for money and power.

The city was very prosperous, but many people lived in misery because a minority kept everything for themselves. Both the rich and the poor were violent and vicious and did not respect the rights of others.

One day a very holy man went to live in the city. He rented a room in a poor neighborhood. He dedicated himself to serving and helping others. He spoke to them of the need to change their lives, and he spent long hours praying for the people. But no one paid him any mind and nothing changed. And the saint was very discouraged.

God became very impatient that the corruption had lasted so long with no improvement. And God considered

47

excluding that city from divine providence. And God sent
an angel to the city to make a report.

An angel went to the city and returned and reported to
God: "Everyone in that city lives as if you did not exist.
No one prays to you. No one thanks you for anything.
They all follow their evil inclinations, and the corruption
is complete. But there is one holy man who does good and
who prays and suffers for others. But no one pays him any
mind."

God thought about this and decided to continue caring
for the city, for the holy man was part of it, and God was
very pleased with this man's life.

As time passed the inhabitants of the city began to
resent the presence of the saint to the point that they could
no longer tolerate him. And one night they kidnapped him
and took him outside the city, and they never heard from
him again. And the city continued as corrupt as ever.

God found out what had happened, reconsidered, and
again sent the angel to report on the situation.

The angel went and returned and reported to God:
"Things are more or less the same as they were before,
and the saint was indeed kidnapped and disappeared. But
there is some interesting news. The fate of the holy man
made an impression on some of his neighbors and on some
of the other families in the city. And some have begun
to follow his example and to change their ways. They are
very few, and they are immersed in a sea of corruption,
but they have begun to pray and to sacrifice for others.
They feel a great communion with everyone, and although
it seems that nobody pays them any mind these people try
to do what the others will not: they pray, they ask your

pardon, and they thank you. They try to be upright and helpful and to follow your paths, compensating for what the others fail to do. But they see few results, and they get discouraged.

God again thought about this and decided to continue caring for the city, for those faithful people were a part of it, and God was very pleased with their lives. And these people compensated for the vices and the blindness of the others. And this gave God hope that one day the city would change.

———— Θ ————

In many places the Church is a minority, a "tiny remnant" in the midst of unbelief. In other places good Christians are a tiny remnant within a blind and immoral society.

There is a temptation to be discouraged and to wonder what purpose the Church serves. What use is prayer and faith and love? Why sacrifice for others and what good is Christian witness?

Perhaps our idea of the mission of the Church and Christianity in the world is too results-oriented, too "operational." Perhaps we have an operational idea of the mission of Christ.

To understand Jesus we need to remember that he was the culmination of the "tiny remnant" of Israel, that he represented the whole people before God and that he compensated with his fidelity for the treachery of Israel. In his preaching, loving others, and giving his life Jesus represents not only Israel but the whole human race. And he reconciles us to God. The life and death of Jesus are not for himself, but for others, representing others.

This representation of the blind and sinful multitude by a faithful tiny remnant has been conferred on the Church by Christ. Charged with the reconciling mission of Jesus, the Church and Christians live not only for visible results in the apostolate (which, of course, they try to achieve). Rather, they "are" and live as representatives before God of what others do not live but should.

The prayer of praise, of pardon, and of thanksgiving of a Christian community represents and compensates for the prayer that others should offer and do not, the prayer that creation cannot offer. The Eucharist of believers is the sacrifice that reconciles to God not only those who offer it but also "the multitude." The body offered and the blood spilled are offered "for you and for many for the forgiveness of sins."

The practice of Christian love and sacrifice for others does not always have a visible result. The experience can be frustrating. Everything seems to remain the same, and the disproportion between the meager good that we do and the misery and the evil around us is overwhelming. But again, we must consider the testimony and the commitment of Christians not only for its "operational" value, but also for its "representational" value, representational of the multitude.

A mysterious aspect of the love of God is that God allows for a few to save the many and to compensate for them. That is why the Church places so much importance on the quality of Christian life — on the lives of the saints, on the consecrated life, on the contemplative life, for example — and not merely on its quantitative value. In this sense, an anonymous saint contributes more to the liberation of the world than many mediocre Christians or than the multitude that does not do good.

And one reason why the world is not better is because we Christians, the "representatives," are not better. And so too every profound reform in society, and in the Church as well, requires commitment and holiness in the persons and communities who are responsible for the reforms.

The Parable of
the Mountain Climbers

Two mountain climbers were preparing to scale a peak in the Himalayas. They learned about all the routes and all the dangers of the mountain. They studied the weather and carefully planned their procedures. They trained for an entire year and acquired the best equipment. They hired a guide, and, full of hope, they began the ascent.

Before they left, the guide, who was wise and experienced, recommended that they carry certain pills and a certain brandy. "You will need it," he said. "Above a certain altitude you use up your energy more quickly. If you take one pill a day you will keep your energy level up. This brandy will help you cope with the various changes of climate in the different stages of the journey."

The mountain climbers paid him no mind because they thought that guides are ignorant, superstitious, and given to exaggeration.

They climbed and climbed, and the mountain climbers,

after they passed a certain altitude, began to weaken. The guide took his daily pill and was as strong as ever. At each stage the change in the weather affected them so much that the mountain climbers could not continue. The guide drank his brandy and maintained his positive frame of mind and self-confidence.

After several weeks, the mountain climbers were totally frustrated and decided to return. The path down was broad and easy and they were soon back at their point of departure.

The mountain climbers were very sad because they had failed. The guide was very sad too, because they had not listened to him.

——— Θ ———

The Himalayan trail is the pathway of our life. We are the mountain climbers. The guide is the Church that recommends and offers the sacraments to us.

The sacraments are necessary if we want to climb up the mountain. We do not need them if we are on our way down.

The sacraments renew our life every day as well as at the critical stages of our life itinerary: birth, adolescence, marriage, illness, death.

— 24 —

The Case of
the Jealous Old Woman

A woman was very devoted to Jesus and had a great desire to meet him just like the women in the Gospels who had met Jesus: Mary Magdelene, the Samaritan woman, the woman caught in adultery....

And she was jealous of them.

She had heard that it was possible to meet Jesus here on earth. Even if we do not see Jesus, we can meet him in a tangible way just as the women of the Gospels did. And she began to look for the way to accomplish this.

She hung a crucifix in her room and knelt down before it and began to pray. But this did not satisfy her because the Christ on the cross gave no signs of meeting her.

She read books about Jesus, but this did not satisfy her either, because she could not be sure that the words and deeds of Jesus were personally addressed to her.

She tried to encounter Jesus within herself, but this left her dissatisfied as well, because she could not tell if what she experienced was from her imagination, from the devil, or from her encounter with Jesus.

She tried to find Jesus in others, but the defects in others prevented her from achieving this. She tried to find Jesus in the priest, and she spoke with him about this, but the priest was very busy and the conversation was a disappointment.

Finally she resorted to the sacraments. And she heard Jesus pardon her with real words, and she discovered Jesus giving himself up for her and meeting her in consecrated bread.

And she understood that this mutual encounter in the sacraments was just as real and as personal as that of the women in the Gospels. And like them she began to change her life. And from then on she was no longer jealous of them.

— 25 —

The Quality of Mercy

Mercy has no ideology.
—*Moral of the Parable
of the Good Samaritan*

———— Θ ————

It has been said that it is proper to Christian identity to relativize the social, political, and cultural ideologies that are constantly bombarding us. But it is also said that it is difficult to engage in a social practice, or even a pastoral one, without some mix of ideology. And that even faith, which in itself is not ideology, has ideological elements to it. How can we escape from this vicious circle? How can we deepen our Christian identity?

I looked to Christ for enlightenment, the one whose commitment was total and unambiguous. And I discovered that the source of his commitment was mercy, mercy for all, a mercy partial to every kind of human misery.

And I understood that only a practice whose root is mercy can be free of ideology.

And I realized that Christ's "utopia" was not a model for society; it was rather the Reign of God, and the Reign of God has no ideology.

———— Θ ————

Pardon and mercy are values typical of Christian identity. For some they are very difficult to achieve; for others they are an unreasonable requirement.

I think that when he formulated this ideal Jesus did not have in mind only the commandment of love. Or the consideration that we should pardon others because God continuously pardons us. Jesus also had in mind the reality of human nature. When Jesus asks us to imitate him by pardoning in love, he asks us at the same time to be understanding and merciful toward the moral and psychological fragility of human beings.

We are all psychologically fragile and inconsistent in our behavior. Many of us are victims of neuroses and complexes. Many offenses are not deliberate and culpable, but a mixture of obscure and unconscious motives. We do what we do not want to do. We make people suffer whom we do not want to hurt.

And Jesus loves us as we are, me and others, unconditionally. To pardon is to imitate Jesus in his acceptance of people as they are.

———— Θ ————

We do not pardon because we concentrate on the weaknesses and sins of others, which are real, and thus pardon from our "righteousness." ("I would never do that.")

We are better able to pardon if we understand the extent of our own weakness. If we faced the pressures and temptations that others do, we cannot say that we would not do what others do. The circumstances are always important if we are to understand the sinner.

We know what we should do. We do not know if we would do it if we were put in circumstances that would reveal our vulnerability. To understand this is a form of humility.

And one way God shows us mercy is to preserve us from such situations.

To pray for the needy and suffering is Christian, but it is even more Christian to pray for the rich and the powerful as well.

To pray for our friends and for the victims of evil is Christian; to pray for our enemies and those guilty of evil as well is even more Christian.

The struggle for justice is Christian; but it is more Christian when it is accompanied by a hunger for God and the desire for God's everlasting Reign. And awaiting the fulness of God's Reign is Christian when it is accompanied by the "hunger and thirst for justice" on earth.

— *26* —

The Parable of
the Hidden Liberator

God became a human being and stayed with us.

——— Θ ———

There once was a very wise and very good king who had an only son as heir. The son was as wise and as good as his father, and the people loved him and looked forward to his being king. While he awaited the moment he would be made king, the son traveled to foreign lands to prepare himself better.

The years passed and the old king got sick and died. But first he announced to the people that his son was on his way home.

After the king's death many problems arose in the country, because there was no guide to provide good example. And so the people went to look for the son so he could begin to rule as soon as possible. But they could not find him. They knew that he was to be found somewhere in their midst, but they did not know where. Meanwhile, the situation got worse. Injustices abounded, as did corruption and the spirit of division and competition. And the people longed for the son who had disappeared because they knew that he would free them from their misery.

The search continued, first in the likeliest places, and then throughout the land. One group went to look in the universities, but they did not find him there. But those who went to search became fascinated with the scientific advances that were being made at the universities, and so they stayed there and forgot about the problems of the country and the liberator they were seeking.

Others went to look for the son among the politicians, but they did not find him there. But they became fascinated by power and its possibilities, and so they stayed with the politicians and forgot about everything else. Others sought him in the world of finance, but he was not there either. And they became fascinated by wealth and so remained there and forgot about the rest. Others even went to find him in centers of amusement and vice, and he was not there either. But they became fascinated with so much pleasure, forgot all about the misery of the people and their awaited liberator, and remained there.

But in one of the poorest neighborhoods of the country there was a poor and simple man who was dedicated to helping the needy and to teaching them to overcome their misery and vices and to be happy. Nobody knew where he had come from. And his fame as a holy and wise man increased. And many people began to be guided by him and to imitate him. And people began to come to him from other places as well.

Everyone loved him and trusted him. And then one day the good man revealed to them that he was the heir and liberator they were seeking and the whole neighborhood believed him. And so the people traveled throughout the country to tell others about their discovery. But many were not interested. They had become totally involved in politics, finance, research, vice, amusement....

The people in the poor neighborhood did not get discouraged. Inspired by their guide and liberator, they continued their work to make life in their country just and loving as it had been before.

— 27 —

The Parable of the Filipinos

A scholar decided to study Filipino culture. But he did not believe it was necessary to go to the Philippines, for there were Filipino immigrants in his country and in other neighboring countries.

And so he met many Filipinos and learned something of their culture. But because his contacts were so scattered and the Filipinos he met had been uprooted from their homeland, he was not able to achieve a synthesis nor penetrate the soul of the culture.

And finally he understood that to truly understand the Filipinos and to experience their culture he had to visit their homeland. In the Philippines he was able to understand deeply the Filipinos and their culture. And he realized that his previous work had been fragmentary and superficial and that only now would his research be integrated and valid.

——— Θ ———

The Reign of God is more extensive than the Church. The values of God's Reign can be found in peoples, societies, and cultures that are not influenced by the Church. God's Reign and the Church are not one and the same.

But God's Reign is to be found within the Church. The Church is its privileged place, the homeland of God's Reign. The Church is the synthesis and the fulness of the values of God's Reign, the place where the signs of God's Reign take roots, signs that can be found outside the Church in a fragmentary way.

— *28* —

The Parable of
the Healer

There once was a young woman who had great faith in medications, but she had no faith in the medical profession nor in doctors.

When she got sick she would go the the pharmacy and buy whatever medicine seemed best to her. And so it went. But eventually problems began to arise.

She had an infection, and the medicines she took had serious side effects on her heart, and for these side effects she could find no remedy. Later she suffered from allergies, and she used the medicine that she trusted in. But these too had side effects and her allergies only got worse. As she got older she suffered from migraine headaches, and she took her medicines. The headaches went away for awhile, but eventually they returned to afflict her. Finally she had to take a whole series of medications every day to control her ailments, and all the medication began to take its toll.

So one day she decided to consult a healer who people said had hidden powers that were more effective than doctors and medicines. The healer stopped all her medications and gave her a potion to take every day. And the woman became a great advocate of exotic medicines. Her health seemed to improve, and she was so enthusiastic that she tried to convince her friends to stop seeing their doctors and use the healer's potion.

But eventually all her ailments returned and she became very sick. And the healer and her potions were of no use, and the medications in which she had put all her faith were of no help at all.

And so finally she sent for a doctor, who realized that she was very sick. He did what he could to help her and then had her hospitalized. At first the treatment seemed very long and complicated to the woman, and it was very difficult for her to stop taking her old medications. But finally she began to trust the doctors and she recovered her health.

———— Θ ————

This parable is about people who understand religion in their own way and think there is no need for the Church to guide them and help them.

It is a parable about people who are not at all concerned whether their religious beliefs are authentic and correspond to truth. Or those who have faith in God, in their own way, and believe that is enough. Or about those who accept whatever belief happens to be in fashion or that they chance to come across, but make no effort to verify it with the faith of the Church or church teaching.

The parable is about people who get very excited about

promises of a religious sect, leaving behind the richness of the faith they had had.

And finally, this parable is about people who believe that we can be Christians without the Church. Or that there can be a healthy Christianity with no Church. Or that we can overcome moral misery and human fragility with human science alone, without relying on the spirituality of the Church.

— 29 —

The Parable of
the Wandering Woman

A certain woman found her native city to be very bleak and boring, and she decided to emigrate to other more exciting places, fascinating places that she had heard about.

She arrived in one of the cities she had heard about; she went there because of what she had heard of its fast action and night life. But she could not find work. So she traveled to another country anxious to visit its exotic cities. But she soon realized that she was not accepted there because she was a foreigner.

So she emigrated to another continent, to places famous for their high culture and progress. But she soon became disenchanted of the materialism and lack of moral values. And so she traveled around the world going from one city to the next.

After many years she came to a smaller city, not so rich and dazzling. And she was welcomed there by very friendly people, who helped her find work. There was no violence or vice in the streets, and the people lived very simply but happily.

And the woman realized that this was her home town, changed over the years, but still with the same values that she had become homesick for, values that she had rediscovered during her long journeys.

And so she stayed there.

——— Θ ———

This parable is about people who look for happiness in faraway places and experiences when it is really to be found right at home in our everyday lives. Or about people who seek God in esoteric doctrines and practices, moving from one to another when in fact they could find God in the church on the corner.

This parable is about all those people who abandon their Christian experience because the Church seems inadequate to them, and after a long exodus through other ideas and experiences come to a place that satisfies them — only to discover that this place is the very Church that they had left behind because they had never really known it.

——— Θ ———

The Church is like a good mother who raises her children well. But no matter how hard she tries, she is human and inevitably the upbringing is in some way deficient.

The children receive everything from their mother and accept it as good, uncritically. Above all they receive the desire and the means to grow.

As they grow up the children learn to grow on their own, and they become more critical. And they begin to see the deficiencies of their mother and the limitations of their upbringing. And sometimes there is a break. The children reject everything they have received and look for other criteria and other paths.

Maturity should be the post-critical stage of life. It is the time of synthesis. Adults rediscover the richness of the upbringing they have received, because they have seen and experienced many things. And they are able to compensate for the defects in their upbringing, because their mother has taught them to grow and has given them her principles for discernment.

— 30 —

The Parable of
the Concert

Two young people wanted to hear the music of Bach.

They went to a concert where Bach was being performed.

The place was not the best. The seats were uncomfortable. You could hear the noise from the street. People arrived late, and others left early.

One of the young people was very bothered by these distractions, and they distracted him from the music, even though the music was excellent.

The other was a little distracted at first, but then she began to concentrate on the music and paid no attention to the deficiencies of the concert hall.

After the concert the two returned to their homes. The first had learned nothing of Bach and lost interest in music.

The second enjoyed Bach and continued to cultivate her interest and to enjoy music.

———— Θ ————

Like music, the Church is first of all an experience. It is the place of encounter with God and with others. It is the place of Jesus, of life, and of liberation.

Only when we have had this experience can we understand the Church and speak of it — and criticize its human context.

It is easy to criticize the institutional forms the Church has had throughout history. But we should not forget that the music these forms have produced is like a great torrent coursing through history and humanizing it.

— *31* —

The Case of
the Demanding Convert

There was once a man who wanted to learn about Christianity, because he had heard that it was a religion that came from God. But he had his doubts.

So he went to a church and he was given the Gospels to read. He read them and was very impressed. But then he observed that the Christians he knew lived the Gospels very poorly, and he continued to have his doubts.

He returned to the church and he was invited to participate in a very beautiful liturgy. He did so and was very impressed. But there were many things that he did not understand, and so he still had his doubts.

He again returned, and he was given the documents of Vatican Council II. He read them and was impressed. But since he had also read about the shortcomings of the Church throughout history, he was not convinced.

He was confused and did not return to the church for some time. But then one day he met a holy man and got to know him. And he was very impressed, and all at once he understood the Gospels, the liturgy, and the Church. And he was converted.

————— Θ —————

Over time doctrines and ideologies become inconsistent. They suffer from mediocrity. Their advocates lose their ideals, and their practice contradicts their theory. As time passes, the convictions are accommodated to the practices.

For some the Church is no exception to these laws. The Church has been inconsistent during its long history. Too many Christians are mediocre. So on what basis does the Church claim to be the bearer of divine doctrine and to be a guide that should be followed?

A social or religious institution is evaluated *(a)* by the quality and permanence of its ideals, and *(b)* by the practice of those of its members most closely identified with those ideals. Challenges to the Church usually do not have to do with the quality of its gospel ideals, upheld consistently for centuries. This continuity of ideals, in the oldest institution in the West (if not in the world), is in itself exceptional and suggests divine intervention. There is no other case in history of an institution lasting so long and at the same time upholding intact its first principles.

The challenge is rather addressed to the practice of the Church and its members, at least at certain periods in history. During the two thousand years of church history there are abundant examples. But before we speak of the decline of the institution we should first ask that institution whom it considers to be its most representative and consistent members. Whom does it hold up, even in

its periods of decadence, as models for the others. Whom
does it consider to be living out its ideals faithfully, rising
above the mediocrity of the majority?

Whom does the Church hold up as a model for itself,
always and everywhere? In whom does the Church recognize genuine Christian practice? With whom does the
Church identify? Not with the Christian "majority," nor
with any and every priest, bishop, or pope. For majority opinion or ecclesiastical authority is not sufficient to
identify authentic Christian practice.

When it comes to practice, the Church identifies fully
only with Jesus Christ — and with the saints, be these few
or many.

Why are the saints declared as such by the Church?
Because the saints have demonstrated consistency between
Christian ideals and practice. When the Church declares a
person to be a saint, it is as if it were saying, "This person
has achieved the ideal that I am proposing and that I am
able to live out only rarely in my members."

So the Church has two ways to maintain authenticity
and to inspire human beings: by its gospel teaching, and
by authentic witnesses to that teaching, the people we call
saints. They are yet another proof that the Spirit dwells
in the Church, and that the Church remains incorruptible
through time.

— *32* —

The Parable of
the Disorganized Traffic

Should we first try to change people's hearts, or unjust social institutions?

Θ

In a certain city there were many traffic accidents. So the people brought in experts to reorganize the system of thoroughfares and traffic signals, and the result was that the traffic was very well organized. But there continued to be many accidents, because the people drove with no respect for each other.

So others decided to educate the drivers, and they left the system as it had been. The drivers eventually learned to drive very courteously, and the number of accidents declined. but there were still very many accidents because the organization of the traffic was very poor.

33

The Parable of
the Renters

An apartment was shared by six renters. Their living conditions were most inadequate. The weather in that city was very cold and they had no heat. Running water was rationed, and there was no electricity because the landlord had not had the wires repaired. The kitchen was small and there was not enough time for each renter to take a turn cooking, so that every day one or another had nothing to eat.

The renters were forever in conflict and they quarreled because they all were worried about themselves. They were also quite discouraged because they had no way to resolve the problem of the cold, the water, and the electricity.

Then one of them decided to do something about the situation in the apartment. There were some things she could not do much about. She couldn't change the building, she couldn't change the weather, and she couldn't do anything about the water shortage in the neighborhood. But she did not get discouraged.

She began by convincing the other renters that they had to join together and to help each other and to stop being selfish and competitive. And so they began to share the kitchen and what little water there was. And they were all able to eat well and there was water for everyone. And they also agreed to present a joint complaint to get the electricity repaired, and before long the electricity was repaired.

For now they did not have the power to change the apartment or the neighborhood or the city ordinances. But by changing the relationship among themselves and the values that affected their lives as renters, they were able to solve the problems they were having in living together. They were able to make their lives more human, so that life was no longer so depressing. And they learned to look hopefully at the problems that, for now, they were unable to solve.

———— Θ ————

The Church and evangelization change society. But they do not change the laws, structures, or institutions of society. Rather they change its "soul," the relationships and values among people. Like Jesus, the Church humanizes and creates community.

The function proper to the Church and the Christian religion is not to change economic policies or power relationships (in the face of which, by the way, it is quite impotent). Its function is rather to inject the values of God's Reign into society.

   To change institutions and social structures is the role
of politics and politicians and technicians, and Christians
should participate in the process. To change moral values,
the relationships, and the soul of human beings in society
is the role of the Church and evangelizers.

34

The Parable of
the Airplane

A passenger plane set out on a long trip. Shortly after it left, the passengers began to use the restrooms.

In the restrooms these was a notice that read: "Please leave the restroom clean for those who will use it after you." Some of the passengers tried to do this.

But many of the passengers did not think of others and abused the restrooms. Some used great amounts of paper towels and even took them away with them. Others took soap. Some threw all kinds of things into the toilets, which eventually became clogged.

The plane made a stop, and some passengers got off and others got on. As the journey continued the new passengers used the restrooms, and they discovered that they were dirty and not working properly. There was no soap or paper. Everyone became tense. People stayed in the restrooms for long periods, so others had to wait in long lines, which increased their irritation.

People began to speak rudely to each other and to quarrel about who was first in line. And they began to cause damage to the doors of the restrooms. The frustration and the violence spread. The flight attendants had to stop serving the meals and to suspend the other services.

The plane made another stop and new passengers got on. They walked into a situation of violence in which everyone was worried only about himself or herself. And instead of the pleasant trip they had been looking forward to, they were unable to use the plane's facilities and they were denied their rights as passengers. And their trip was very difficult.

———— Θ ————

How should we understand social sin? The sin of a society unjustly organized, in which the institutions and cultural models generate injustice?

For many the notion is difficult to understand. Sin is an offense against oneself or against others — and by the same token an offense against God, for the glory of God is the good of the human being. And so every sin properly speaking is personal. Only human beings are free, responsible, and capable of doing good or evil.

But the Church also speaks of social sin, as analogous to personal sin and related to it. Personal sins always affect society and family and social relationships, often quite directly and explicitly. These social effects of sin persist even after the person has stopped sinning. They gradually create inhuman conditions that get beyond the control of individuals. The accumulation of social evils, generation after generation, creates situations of collective injustice and dehumanization, aggravated by new sins. No one carries all the blame; the blame is shared by many.

This sharing in social evil is another instance of that mysterious human solidarity in the evil of the world known as original sin. And so perhaps to explain social sin the notion of the accumulation of personal sins in society is not sufficient. We must also realize that original sin is rooted in social relationships and not only in human hearts.

This helps us to understand what is so disturbing about social injustice. If sin, strictly speaking, can be committed only by individuals, only individuals can be converted. Societies as such are not converted; rather they are made more human in the communion of love and justice. Communion in evil is overcome only through communion in good.

There will never be perfect societies. As long as there is sin there will be social sin. Nonetheless we can and we should make our society more human.

Christianity is competent and effective in overcoming personal sin, which has an effect of bringing about a more just and loving practice in social relationships. Under its influence, people can become saints and act like brothers and sisters in their social world. History and our own experience demonstrate this.

But Christianity is not competent or so effective in directly transforming the structures or institutions of societies. History and our own experience show this as well. For this would mean to uproot original sin from society, which is impossible. Original sin is uprooted by baptism and grace, and only individuals (not societies) can be baptized and sanctified.

So it makes no sense to say that Christianity has failed because after so many centuries social evil has not been eliminated from Christian countries. Christianity has not failed to make social relationships more human, to offer persons a path of personal liberation despite social evil.

35

The Case of
the Reconciled Prophet

There once was a city that was rife with social injustice. And there was a priest there who gave lectures about justice. In these talks he very clearly denounced the inequalities in society.

And after one of these lectures someone challenged him: "What you say is very true, but you ought to be talking to others, the ones who are responsible for the injustice. They're the ones who need to be challenged and condemned so that they change. It's the rich people in the city you should be talking to, and they're the least sensitive of all."

And the priest answered: "You are right. This is exactly what I want to say to the rich, to denounce their abuses and their insensitivity. But I still do not feel that I am ready to do this. Since I was very young I've been prejudiced against the rich and have felt very hostile toward them. And I've still not got beyond this. The day that I love the rich as I love you I will feel prepared to approach them and to denounce their insensitivity and their responsibility for the social evils of the city. That's the only way that they will accept me and change their lives."

36

The Parable of
the Dissatisfied People

In a certain country there was a severe economic crisis and there were shortages of everything. The people were very unhappy.

An angel came and asked the people what they needed to be happy, because the angel would give it to them.

Some asked for the ability to satisfy all their needs. The angel granted this. These people went about acquiring many things, but since their aspirations and needs were forever on the increase, they were never happy.

Others asked the angel to give them the freedom to decrease their needs. And the angel granted this. And those people lived very austerely, but they were happy.

———— Θ ————

On a recent trip to India I spent a few days in Kondivita village, an ancient and typical rural village of West India, now absorbed by the spreading city. I was the guest of an enchanting and numerous Indian family, who were Christians, and who keep up a great old house built in the last century.

I visited a few neighbors. (In India it is not proper that guests who are ministers of religion not make a courtesy visit to the neighboring friends of the family with which they are staying.) The family friends are gracious and hospitable in the same way as the poor people of Latin America.

But the poverty in which they live is more startling, not so much in terms of deterioration and misery, as of austerity and nakedness. Their shacks quite often have only one room, do not have chairs, or high tables, or the electric devices that are common among the poor peoples of the West. It is a poverty of economic scarcity combined with austerity and divestiture. (Later I discovered that in many countries of the East there is almost no importation of mechanical and electrical devices, such as washing machines, so that unemployment, which is already severe, might not increase through the automation of work.) In the meantime they do not seem to need or to miss the household articles that I am accustomed to use.

They sit comfortably on the floor in the Hindu fashion, and this makes chairs unnecessary. They do not use mattresses or complicated beds. They are perfectly accustomed to sleep on mats and would be very uncomfortable sleeping any other way. Closets, dressers, etc. are minimal, and they quickly wash what they have worn or will be wearing. The women are unaffected by the costly problem of fashion and its changes. They use a sari for all occasions and seasons. They earn almost nothing, if in fact they have a job; but they evidently spend almost nothing for the needs of life.

They eat very little, at least in my view, with often only one regular meal a day, snacking here and there. After some days of adhering to this dietary plan, I began to wonder if this was not all that an adult needs to eat each day. Perhaps after a certain age a human being begins to eat more than necessary, being habituated to doing so by consumerism and the pleasures of eating. Seeing so many poorly nourished children, I became convinced that the problem of world hunger is based not only on the shortfall of supply, but on poor distribution, on the fact that one part of humanity has hardly anything to eat while the other part eats excessively. Hunger is of course a relative and cultural phenomenon. But it must be asked whether the three of four daily meals consumed in the Western world are really necessary.

In effect, my friends in Kondivita village seem to have resolved the problem of development in an original way: they do not satisfy every need, real or artificial; rather they reduce their needs and control them. This could be a way towards humanization and growth, if we agree with the testimony of the saints, the monks, and the ascetics, which in all religions constitutes a way (an extraordinary way, it must be recognized) of human liberation.

However, in the case of our Indian friends we must not fool ourselves. The majority are neither saints nor ascetics, and the way of life they lead is imposed on them by poverty. There are many real necessities that they are unable to satisfy. (Think only of health needs and education.) Perhaps many of the so-called necessities that are part of life in developed countries are not felt by them. This is typical of extreme poverty. But it does not mean that they are not called to satisfy their needs in order to achieve fulness of life.

These people cannot present themselves as ideal models of human development; to the contrary, the asceticism that they practice has an air of dehumanization and even of alienation. Asceticism requires profound spirituality. It is always the activity of a minority, and when it is practiced on a massive scale it becomes highly suspicious. But, in the midst of everything, there is an important and redeemable dimension of liberation in the way of life of an Indian village.

———— Θ ————

Several weeks later, when I left India, I had the opportunity to stop in New York. I stayed in the apartment of a friend. Arriving from India, the contrast overwhelmed me. It was not so much the difference between poverty and wealth, but the contrast between two philosophies of development.

The apartment of my friend was bursting with furniture, utensils, and the latest electric devices offering efficiency and comfort. Instructed by my previous experience, I began to ask myself to what extent this multitude of things was necessary for human development, and whether it actually represented progress in the quality of living. I made an inventory of the latest devices I encountered, and I found that the great majority were not designed to better the quality of life, but to provide greater comfort — the saving of a few seconds, the avoidance of a movement or change in temperature. Some were simply luxury items which go out of fashion or end up not being practical. What kind of development is this that diminishes the capacity to resist the harshness of life, to have control over oneself, and to accept certain austerities as part of the human condition?

Faced with the use and consumption of so many superfluous things that have come to be considered necessary in the life of the so-called First World, and that constitute the framework of a way of conceiving development that is unilateral and dehumanizing, I thought back to the shacks of the Indians. While the Indians have a relatively small number of needs to fill, the people here are continually conscious of more needs than they ought to feel. The New Yorkers earn a great deal of money, but spend more. Paradoxically, their budgets are as stretched as those who earn hardly anything and spend hardly anything. Although they enjoy greater comforts and can indulge more whims, the price they pay is the elimination of any form of asceticism in their daily lives.

Theirs is a pattern of life and development that cannot be imitated by the majority of peoples on the planet, the so-called Third and Fourth Worlds, nor would this be in their best interest. Taking everything into consideration, my friends of Kondivita village, despite their poverty, have no desire to share the level and manner of life of a middleclass New Yorker.

It would then seem that the majority of the ideologues of development and of the struggle against poverty seem to be trapped between two equally frustrating viewpoints: either one tolerates a dehumanizing poverty often under the

guise of a pseudo-asceticism, or one embarks upon an in-
definite search for greater well-being and comfort that the
rich countries have decided to call "progress" and "development," and that they try to present as such to the rest of
the planet. On this point the similarities among the cap-
italisms, the state socialisms, and the Marxisms are sur-
prisingly strong. Although they have different ideological
and social concerns, they have in common an exacerbated
economic model that forces them to forget and sometimes
to disdain the culture and religion of the nations.

Latin America, perhaps more than any other area, because of its Western and "newly prosperous" character,
is caught in this dilemma. On the one hand, it desires
the type of development of the First World, without the
slightest hope that its poor majority will be able to take
part in it. On the other hand, it has a cultural and religious substratum that is profoundly "humanistic" and, for
that reason, stands in opposition to this. In face of this
dilemma, many Christian thinkers and preachers seem to
offer only a false economistic alternative, with its related
type of liberation. They seem to reject any "third way"
proposals, reducing them to one of the previous alternatives.

Perhaps they are correct if the "third way" is again ideological and economistic. But others conceive of a "third
way" that is a leavening represented by the social doctrine
of Christianity. It seems to me that Christian social doctrine completely changes the rules of the game and the
definition of the problem. It offers a new humanism and
conception of life, including the quality of life, and the
motives for which one continues to live. It can help my

friends in Kondivita village and also my friends in New York, redeeming what is of value in their respective attitudes towards life.

What inspires us in this authentic Christian humanism is the teaching that asceticism and austerity are dimensions of true development. Through a spirituality of relativizing progress and material well-being, it is close to the best religious tradition of India. Paradoxically, in order to escape from poverty, whether it be the through the redistribution of wealth or through self-advancement, it is necessary to know how to practice poverty. Liberation is not merely the satisfaction of needs. It is also moderating and controlling both needs and expectations. Progress based on unlimited comfort and infinite production of goods and services cannot bring an authentic socioeconomic liberation. Only a degree of austerity and the application of restraint, in the personal and the collective realm, can bring such a change. In a nutshell, any valid plan of development and social or personal liberation must be in harmony with the ultimate purpose and motivation of human life.

— *37* —

The Parable of
the Hospital

A remote village in the hinterland had no doctor, no medicines, no hospital. The people suffered greatly from this lack of health care, and there were many who were hopelessly ill.

Most of the people were very poor and so did not have the means to go the city for health care. But there were also some wealthy families that, despite the lack of health services in the village, were easily able to travel to the city to take care of themselves.

And then one day a group of missionaries arrived in the village. Soon they had built a hospital, small but well staffed and well equipped, where everything was free, and anyone could go there, whether rich or poor.

The day the hospital was to be opened, everyone was present, and the missionary told them, "Happy today are the poor and suffering of the village, for this hospital is for you..."

The following day a group of the richest people in the village went to speak to the missionary and to ask him why he had referred only to the poor, excluding everybody else, since the hospital was supposed to be for everyone.

And the missionary said to them, "It is true that the hospital is for everyone, including you, and everyone will be taken care of free of charge and courteously. But it is also true that for those who are poorest and in greatest need this hospital is good news of great joy in a special way, for, unlike you, they have had no other place to go. And that is why now they are especially happy, and why when we built the hospital we have had them especially in mind, without excluding anyone.

—— Θ ——

"Blessed are the poor, because the Reign of God is theirs."

The Reign of God is of everybody and for everybody. God's Reign is offered in a special way to the poor, not because they are better, but rather because for them the coming of God's Reign is especially good news.

The Parable of
the Sick Brother

A mother had five children. Four were healthy and one was sickly.

She loved all her children very much, but she was especially concerned about and affectionate toward the sickly one. Moreover she taught her four healthy children to have this same concern and preference for their sickly brother.

They all loved each other very much, but the weakest child was everyone's favorite, and no one was jealous.

——— Θ ———

The preferential option for the poor: God loves everyone in a nonexclusive way, but God has a preference for the weakest and most oppressed children. And God has taught all of us to have this same attitude toward each other — just as the four healthy children learned from their mother to have a preferential love for their sick brother.

The Parable of
the Two Moralities

In a certain totalitarian country two young friends were sitting in a café having a discussion about ethics and moral principles. One was a member of the Party and was a non-believer; the other was a believer.

The non-believer said, "There is no need to have religion to have moral principles. My ideological education provides me with the moral values that you have: justice, work, solidarity, austerity.... The leaders of the Party insist that I be consistent with our ideology, and their criticisms help me. I don't need religious motivation. I can't see what religion can add to our social ideals...."

After awhile they left together to catch the train to their homes. The train was packed, and the conductor did not even realize they had got on. Nevertheless, the believer went up to the conductor and paid for his ticket; the other did not. When they got off the non-believer asked the believer, "Why did you pay when we didn't have to?"

The believer answered, "That's what religion adds to your morality: to do what is right even though nobody asks you to and nobody sees you."

———— Θ ————

Is it possible to have moral principles and to practice them without religion?

Agnostics and ideologues say that they do not need religious values — and much less religious authority — to live according to ethical principles. And they point to the example of non-believers who uphold a morality of family, of work, of human rights, of justice for the poor.

Believers say that the answer to the question is yes and no. The experience of a morality without religious beliefs needs to be complemented with our experience of the inadequacy of that morality and with the parallel that we see in every society between a lack of religion and moral degradation.

On the one hand it is very difficult to find a person, no matter what that person's religion, without moral principles. We acquire moral principles through education (especially family education), or through our culture (for every culture has ethical models), or through the society we live in (for every society recognizes certain ways of living together). Whether or not we recognize it, all of these imply religious roots: Western civilization with its secular ethical models employs criteria and behavior whose origin is to be found in religion.

If we interpret this from the standpoint of faith, we have to add that the existence of a morality for most people comes from the presence of the Spirit of God in all human beings, and that they are endowed with a moral conscience oriented toward the good and reflecting the law of God. It has been written, and rightly so, that "the human soul is naturally Christian."

On the other hand, moral values of a purely cultural or ideological origin have demonstrated their serious deficiencies. In the first place their ethic is selective. Cultures, societies, ideologies, have their favorite values and their favorite "sins," while they are blind or permissive in other areas of morality. This changes according to the times, the cultural trends, and the prevailing ideologies. These changes are reflected in morality, which is therefore changeable and partial and favors or ignores particular moral values according to the situation. And so marriage and family morality waxes or wanes; ethics in work or the economy are important according to the culture or ideology. Human rights are understood differently according to the societal models and are applied in a discriminatory and partial way.

The inadequacies of secular ethical systems are due to their inadequate moral basis: duty, fidelity to history, work, community, etc. What is peculiar to a religious morality, on the other hand, is that it is based on love.

The religion of love enables a morality to be integral, to maintain all humanizing values and consider all the dimensions of the human being. It also allows morality to achieve complete development, and to be independent of cultural or ideological manipulations.

Secular ethical systems have what is reasonable as an objective. Christian morality has radical love as an objective. The secular systems seek justice, but they have no room for pardon, mercy, or the elimination of vengeance. They practice sacrifice, but they do not have room for gratuitousness or for sacrifice for any reason beyond their "cause" or the horizon of their interest.

40

The Parable of
the Unprejudiced Family

There once was a very large and very close family. All of them had received an excellent upbringing, but they had come to believe that much of what they had learned was anachronistic prejudices or alienations that diminished their freedom. And so both parents and children held to the philosophy of seeking first of all their own personal fulfillment.

The father enjoyed betting on the houses at the track, even though he lost more than he could afford. The mother liked to party and to socialize with younger men, for that made her feel like a self-fulfilled woman. The children had their amusements as well, which made them feel liberated: one smoked marijuana with his friends; another went to live with a movie star; another traveled and enjoyed herself with borrowed money. And all of them felt fulfilled and free of prejudices.

The time passed, and finally the father had brought

the family to bankruptcy with his gambling. His wife left him to run off with a younger man, who in turn left her to run off with a teenage girl. One child was a slave to marijuana, while another was a slave to the movie star, who treated him like a plaything. The third child had no friends, because she could not pay her debts.

And the family that had been so close was destroyed.

---- Θ ----

Christian morality coincides with the fulness of humanization and leads us to that fulness.

Things are moral or immoral not because Christianity says so, but because they humanize or dehumanize, and that is why Christianity calls them moral or immoral.

The moral orientations of the Church are good not because the Church teaches them, but rather the Church teaches them because they are good and humanizing. And the prohibitions of the Church are bad not because the Church prohibits them, but rather the Church prohibits them because they are bad and dehumanizing.

What is important for humanizing life and living it to its fulness is not our personal self-fulfillment in all things, for this is not always within our control. Events are imposed on us and frustration is inevitable.

What is important if we are to live life to its fullest is to give meaning to everything in our lives, including the things that life imposes on us.

And so to understand Christian morality we must understand the true meaning of life, beyond immediate personal self-fulfillment.

41

The Parable of the People Who Did Not Want to Be Happy

One day God took the form of a man and came to earth, because God realized that many people were not happy. And God wanted to communicate to all the people the happiness that God had always had.

As God went about the earth, God saw that indeed few people were genuinely happy, but God was surprised to see that very few people were really seeking happiness. Most people could be divided into two groups: those who were "content" and those who were not "content."

Those who were content had been able to satisfy their main desires. They earned good money, they lived comfortably, they enjoyed the pleasures and vices that they wished. Some enjoyed success, influence, or power. But they did not seem to be interested in true happiness, nor to consider seriously whether they were truly happy or not, nor what true happiness really is.

Those who were not content had not been able to satisfy all their desires, and they aspired to live like the people who were content. They did not seek true happiness either, but rather only to be content. And they were all deaf to the message of true happiness.

And God realized that as long as the people sought only to be "content" they would never find true happiness. And so God began to preach to the contented and the discontented about true happiness, trying to arouse their interest and to lead them out of the blindness of their content.

And many listened, and achieved true happiness, and were no longer so concerned about being "content."

———   Θ   ———

God desires our happiness, insofar as it is possible in this life, and not merely that we be "content." We continuously confuse happiness with contentment. Happiness has a profoundly human, spiritual, and moral character. It has to do with an interior plenitude. It is not incompatible with suffering, physical evil, scarcity, or the non-fulfillment of earthly expectations.

Contentment, on the other hand, comes through pleasure and the satisfaction of immediate temporal goals. Contentment is of short duration and cannot give us fulfillment. Too many people seek contentment and not happiness. Worse yet, too many people are not even interested in true happiness, which always requires moral and spiritual progress, and prefer to live in the pursuit of a spurious contentment.

True happiness is like true freedom and authentic liberation. Few people want to be free, and few people want true liberation, to be the protagonists of their own lives and histories. Many prefer to live with the security and contentment that is as false as it is enslaving.

— *42* —

The Parable of Extinguished Love

Love comes from God.
                    —*1 John 4:7*

——— Θ ———

Human beings had been told that they were able to see each other and all the objects of creation because everything emits light and because this light irradiated by human beings and all things comes from the sun. They had been told that the sun is the only source of this light and all other things project the light of the sun.

But the human beings did not believe this and instead believed that each of them and each of the objects in the world had its own light. And so they asked the sun to leave, since they had no need for it anymore.

And so the sun left, and the earth became dark and the people were not able to distinguish any object nor could they see each other.

——— Θ ———

Human beings had also been told that all love comes from God. But the people paid no attention to this because they saw that they could love without being concerned about God. Young people continued to fall in love, married couples continued to love each other, just as parents loved their children and children loved their parents. Friendships continued to grow and there were very faithful and loyal friends. There were people who worked together who were very close in their ideals and struggles.

And so they told God to take away divine love from the earth, because they did not need it. Men and women were able to love of their own accord, for everyone has the ability and the desire to love.

So God took divine love away from the earth.

And the people continued to fall in love and get married. But little by little they began to seek their own self-fulfillment and not the happiness of the other.

And finally the love of couples became an encounter of mutual selfishness.

Parents became possessive and domineering, and the children could no longer get along with their parents so they left home as soon as they could.

Friendships continued, but now they were motivated only by self-interest or good times; no longer was there any concern for loyalty and much less was there sacrifice for friends.

And those who worked and struggled together joined in solidarity only to confront common dangers and for everything else they used each other to get ahead.

And there was nothing but a caricature of love left on
earth. For human beings continued to have the desire to
love, but they no longer knew how to do it.

———   Θ   ———

When we say, "If it's not cloudy tomorrow, it will be
sunny," everyone agrees, but in fact we have not said much.
What is important is not to agree with such an assertion,
but rather to assure that it will not be cloudy so that it
will be sunny.

Likewise if we say, "It is good to love one another, and
if we love one another more the world will be better," everyone will be in agreement (every religion, every system,
every government). The problem, however, is not to agree
on the truth of the assertion, but rather to find a way to
make it come about.

What is original and proper to Christianity is not the
teaching that it is good to love one another. Wise people
and religious leaders before Christ and after have been
saying that. What is original and proper to the religion
of Jesus is to have made it possible to achieve this ideal,
to have revealed to us that love comes from God and that
this love came into the world through Jesus.

— 43 —

The Parable of the Woman
Who Learned to Evangelize

By way of conclusion, here is a Gospel parable. The Gospel is the Parable of parables. It sums up human and religious experience alike. It sums up the parable of our own lives. It sums up the core of the Christian quest.

————— Θ —————

Jesus left Judea and started back for Galilee again. He had to pass through Samaria, and his journey brought him to a Samaritan town named Shechem.... This was the site of Jacob's well. Jesus, tired from his journey, sat down at the well.

The hour was about noon. When a Samaritan woman came to draw water, Jesus said to her, "Give me a drink." The Samaritan woman said to him, "You are a Jew. How can you ask me, a Samaritan and a woman, for a drink?"

Jesus replied: "If only you recognized God's gift and who it is that is asking you for a drink, you would have asked him instead and he would have given you living water."

"Sir," she challenged him, "you do not have a bucket and this well is deep. Where do you expect to get this flowing water? Surely you do not pretend to be greater than our ancestor Jacob, who gave us this well and drank from it with his sons and his flocks?"

Jesus replied: "Everyone who drinks this water will be thirsty again. But whoever drinks the water I give him will never be thirsty; no, the water I give shall become a fountain within him, leaping up to provide eternal life."

The woman said to him, "Give me this water, sir, so that I shall not grow thirsty and have to keep coming here to draw water."

He said to her, "Go, call your husband, and then come back here." "I have no husband," replied the woman. "You are right in saying you have no husband!" Jesus exclaimed. "The fact is, you have had five, and the man you are living with how is not your husband. What you said is true."

"Sir," answered the woman, "I can see you are a prophet. Our ancestors worshipped on this mountain, but you people claim that Jerusalem is the place where men ought to worship God."

Jesus told her: "Believe me, woman, an hour is coming when you will worship the Father neither on this mountain nor in Jerusalem. . . . Yet an hour is coming, and is already here, when authentic worshippers will worship the Father in Spirit and truth. Indeed, it is just such worshippers the Father seeks. God is Spirit, and those who worship him must worship in Spirit and truth."

The woman said to him: "I know there is a Messiah coming. When he comes, he will tell us everything." Jesus replied, "I who speak to you am he. ..."

The woman then left her water jar and went off into the town. She said to the people: "Come and see someone who told me everything I ever did! Could this not be the Messiah?" At that they set out from the town to meet him. ...

Many Samaritans from that town believed in him on the strength of the woman's word of testimony: "He told me everything I ever did." The result was that, when these Samaritans came to him, they begged him to stay with them awhile. So he stayed there two days, and through his own spoken word many more came to faith. As they told the woman: "No longer does our faith depend on your story. We have heard for ourselves, and we know that this really is the Savior of the world."

Gospel of Saint John, chapter 4

Evangelization demands the testimony of fraternal love

The Gospel account tells us that Jesus had to return from Judea to Galilee; to do that he had to cross Samaria. For Jews, Samaria was a hostile territory through which they passed only in case of necessity, avoiding by all means communication with the Samaritans. At first glance, it does not seem an appropriate place for Jesus to exercise his mission. It was midday in the desert. Tired and thirsty, Jesus sat down at the edge of the well of Shechem, which tradition related to the patriarch Jacob.

As was customary, a woman from the town went out for her water supply. By the context of the account, we know that the story refers to a common, ordinary Samaritan woman. Jesus, without any prejudice, asks her simply for a drink. The woman is surprised and amazed. She had various reasons for being surprised.

The Jew who was seated at the well addressed himself to her. According to the culture and custom he was not supposed to do so. It was surprising not only because she was a woman (women were ignored by men in public places), but also because she was a Samaritan (the Jews discriminated against the Samaritans and did not communicate with them).

Moreover, the Jew asked her a favor: "Give me a drink." Not only did he address her; he also fraternized with her and humbled himself before her. To receive a service from a Samaritan woman ought to have been humiliating.

For Jesus, there was nothing abnormal or artificial in what he had done. It was simply his way. He made no exceptions of anyone; he did not discriminate against women, and the Samaritans formed part of his fraternal and universal love. His manner was so natural that it captured the admiration and interest of the woman of the desert. She opened up to this Jew, who had asked her for a drink. Communication was established, and the affection of the Samaritan woman was won. Jesus perceived this and initiated a long dialogue with her. The dialogue was an evangelical one; under the sun of the desert, Jesus was going to evangelize the woman.

Evangelization was made possible because with his attitude Jesus had created a propitious atmosphere. He had made the woman feel her value and dignity. He had destroyed the prejudices and barriers and had thus given the Samaritan woman the security of fraternal love. In short, the evangelical dialogue was made possible because Jesus accompanied it with his testimony.

Before the woman at the well, Jesus did not "seek" to give testimony in a manner that was planned and artificial. He was simply himself, acting naturally; hence he gave authentic witness.

The authenticity and efficacy of Christian testimony lie in the fact that the witnesses ordinarily are not aware of their testimony. They act naturally and therefore attract; dialogue ensues, all the more profound because it does not demonstrate anything planned or premeditated (a "pose"), but manifests the values of a great love that form a normal part of being and acting.

Dialogue and change

The long dialogue of Jesus with the Samaritan woman is a parable of the missionary dialogue, or of evangelization. What happens in that relatively brief scene at the well is what happens to people, to groups, and to ourselves in the long process of evangelization.

The evangelizer here is Jesus himself. His attitude teaches us several things, which are later verified in the best missionary experience of the Church.

Evangelization is a long process (it may take years) which, before it culminates in the conversion to Jesus in the faith of the Church, passes through small conversions and openings to truth. We are not Christians all at once. We learn to be Christian, and this is the process of our Christian life. We are not missionaries all of a sudden; we learn, step by step, to be more efficient missionaries.

The announcement of the gospel is efficient when it takes into account the reality, the ordinary life, and the human experience of people, in other words, when the culture of a people is considered — their values, their norms, their root-ideas. To evangelize is to enter into dialogue, of the most profound kind, with a given mentality and with a given culture.

This is what Jesus did with the woman of the desert. He started talking to her about water and thirst, something that the woman knew well since they were part of her reality, her ordinary life, and her culture. From there, he opens her heart to greater realities: the living water that quenches thirst forever, with no need to come back to look for it each day.

Evangelization leads to successive conversions in people. It leads them to change little by little in the great things of ordinary life. This is a long process we also perceive in the dialogue by Jacob's well, a parable in the life of each one of us. The woman experiences several changes and conversions.

First, a conversion takes her away from the routine and purely material concern of fetching water every day and of the ordinary chores of her life toward things more valuable — the gift of God, living water. The woman opens herself to this perspective, though still in an imperfect and egoistic manner ("give me of that water so that I may not suffer any more thirst nor have to go back to fetch").

Second, she experiences a conversion in her life of human love. This is the next step that Jesus takes when he refers to her husband. Through it he makes her see that it is not so simple to receive the gift of God and the living water, for it presupposes and at the same time demands that she change her life in everything that is wrong (her married and conjugal life). The woman accepts the challenge: she does not lie to Jesus ("I don't have a husband"), and later on, she does not defend herself.

Third, she experiences a conversion in her religiosity. The woman was religious like her contemporaries, but her religiosity was full of ignorance and wrong conceptions. Jesus leads her into a more perfect religiosity, that of adoring God in spirit and in truth. He helps her to give less importance to exterior routine ("to adore on this hill or in Jerusalem") and to value the interior, spiritually authentic attitude.

Fourth, there is a conversion and an opening to others and to service to them. With this the evangelization of the Samaritan woman matures; she herself is converted into an evangelizer of others. But this deserves a separate reflection.

Contemplation: the fruit of evangelization

The dialogue by the well signifies that Jesus "chose" the Samaritan woman. He found her to evangelize her. The long road to evangelization composed of dialogues, crises, and conversion culminates when Jesus reveals himself to her face to face and she recognizes the Christ in this Jew, believes in him, and becomes his disciple.

The Samaritan woman found the true God in spirit and in truth. She experienced the presence and love of God in her ordinary life. She found the living God. She accepted the gift of God that is "the living water that quenches thirst forever."

The woman of the desert now saw Jesus with new eyes, the eyes of faith, the eyes of contemplative experience. This experience transformed her life — her religious life, her moral life, her relationship with others. The Samaritan woman had become a Christian. This brings to us various missionary teachings:

Mission does not reach its fulness, does not mature as such, if it does not bring people to an explicit conversion to the person of Jesus and makes of them his disciples. Mission is a process; it is a long and complicated process of total liberation from servitude and social, moral, cultural, and even religious pressures. But in the midst of all these dimensions of total liberation, the decisive liberation and the most enriching effect of mission is the encounter with and the following of Jesus, the Christian experience of faith.

Christian experience, the experience of the God of Jesus, is in itself liberating and humanizing. It does not only serve to motivate the other aspects of liberation; it is in itself a personal and collective liberation. The experience of faith does not only "accompany" the other commitments and human experiences; it is worthy in itself, it is at the root of human transformation.

Evangelization leads to properly religious Christian experience, which is a contemplative experience. Evangelization creates contemplatives insofar as it brings one to an authentic experience of the God of Jesus. This is what Jesus calls "the gift of God."

This "gift of God," which mission offers, this experience like "the living water that quenches thirst forever," is offered absolutely to all, but preferentially to the simple and poor of spirit (Matt. 11:25ff). It was offered here by the well in the desert to a townswoman, ignorant and simple, to a woman preoccupied with daily chores, to a woman with a questionable married life, submerged in the errors and judgments of her "popular religiosity."

To us, Jesus' activity by the well may appear to be a waste of time and a wastefulness of the profundity of his doctrine. It seems that he could have kept himself for a more important person. But Jesus makes us see that it is truly the ordinary people who are called to an experience of God. For all of us, there is a time of grace that we should be able to grasp. To the Samaritan woman this "time" came at midday, by Jacob's well. All of us have our hour, a Jacob's well in life.

"The woman then left the water jug and went off into the town...." The Samaritan woman became so enthusiastic and so "captured" by this encounter, that she forgot the jug (unforgivable for a woman who usually went to the well every day) and had no other thought but to run to town to tell everybody about her experience.

To share our faith in Jesus

Her encounter, her conversion, her experience of Jesus made the Samaritan woman automatically, so to speak, a missionary. This was not so much the product of a reflection, or of a well-thought out decision, as it was a necessity. It was something much stronger than she that impelled her to "forget the jug" and "to run to town" to share with the people what she had discovered. She created in the people the same disquiet that Jesus had created in her. She stirred interest among her friends in knowing Jesus and in listening to him to the point that these same people, and not only she, invited Jesus to stay. Thus many believed and changed their lives because of the missionary words of the woman.

The story helps us to understand evangelization in its simplest and most basic level, that which is within the reach of every Christian in our daily ordinary lives.

In the first place, the experience of faith or Christian prayer in general is meant to be shared. Christian contemplation is not authentic unless it creates a dynamism of charity that impels us to share.

This sharing of the Christian experience is evangelization. In its essence, in its core, to evangelize is to share the experience of Jesus Christ. A Christian is at, or goes to, a certain place as a missionary, first and foremost, to share with others the experience of Jesus — especially with others who do not know this experience.

Mission carries out many different tasks; it is complex. It implies fighting for justice and assuming the cause of the poor; it implies knowing and immersing oneself in a culture; it implies creating a church community that celebrates the kingdom of God that is already within it. All this has a missionary meaning and effect because it reveals somehow the experience of the God of Jesus.

Mission, in its simplest act of sharing, is not something

artificially superimposed on life and on the duties of an ordinary Christian. Without going into the more elaborate forms of mission — for instance, to leave one's milieu and culture, to dedicate time and special services to evangelization, things that indeed are also necessary — all Christians can evangelize in our families, in our work, among our friends, and in our neighborhoods as the Samaritan woman did. In this sense we can say that a Christian is a 'born evangelizer," meaning that sharing one's faith and Christian experience with others is something natural, something necessary for a Christian.

We usually share with others that which we have discovered and that which we believe can also enrich or help them. We do this in our day-to-day life. We share and recommend a medicine that helped us get well; we recommend an interesting book, or a person helpful in this or that situation. To evangelize is to share and recommend the greatest riches we have, that which changed and humanized us, that which gave a new meaning to our whole life: our faith in Jesus Christ.

This is why mission is not an imposition. To share and to recommend a value that we have found is not to impose. It is simply not being selfish, not keeping to oneself something that one knows is made for all, that can help and liberate everyone, and that can make everybody happy.

Finally, we cannot evangelize if we do not have any Christian experience to transmit. We evangelize in the measure that we are evangelized. We grow in missionary efficacy in the measure that we deepen our Christian experience. This is a permanent task. We keep on learning to be Christians; we keep on learning to be missionaries.

When she ran to town, the Samaritan woman did not as yet have much to share. As a disciple of the Lord she still had a long way to go but she felt responsible to share what she already had. She found Jesus as a gift of God, and she could not but communicate to others what she had found. This was sufficient. At that moment, God did not ask for more. That is why "many Samaritans believed in him because of the woman's words."

Jesus in the Church

At the beginning, the Samaritans of Shechem believed in Jesus "by the words of the woman." But later they believed in him not because of what she had told them, but because they themselves heard and experienced Jesus, who stayed with them two days.

As a missionary, the role of the Samaritan woman was to make her companions uneasy with respect to Jesus, and above all to put them in contact with him. In the last analysis, therefore, the one who evangelized the people of Shechem was not the Samaritan woman but Jesus himself. The decisive experience that convinced them came as they themselves found and heard Jesus.

The main actor of mission in that town was Jesus; the secondary actor was the woman. Her role, however, was necessary to establish contact between Jesus and the people. This done, she had in some way fulfilled her mission.

We find anew in the account fundamental elements of mission.

To convert, to give life to faith, to bring others to the authentic experience of God and to the liberating service of all people, goes beyond purely psychological, political, or pedagogical means of action. Only the Spirit of Jesus can carry on the missionary task to its fullness. Jesus Christ not only is the first evangelizer but is decidedly and profoundly the only evangelizer. We join him in his evangelical mission; we also evangelize, convinced that he is at work in people's hearts even before our missionary presence, and assured that his Spirit reaches farther and deeper than what our means or action can reach.

The primary function of the evangelizer, therefore, is to facilitate the contact of people with Jesus, his Spirit, his gift of the "living water." Missionary activity, from the simplest form, such as sharing in ordinary life as Jesus does with the Samaritan woman, to the most complex, such as the founding of a church community where once it did not exist, makes use of means of action that in themselves do not lead to the experience of faith, but rather lead to an encounter with the word of God and the action of the Spirit — in short, with the forms in which Jesus here and now comes in contact with the people in order to evangelize them.

Where is Jesus to be found today as source of "living water"? Where does Jesus act today as evangelizer?

At this point, the "well" of the parable becomes most relevant. The well was the meeting-place of Jesus and the woman; it is a symbol as well. In this Gospel, the well of Jacob symbolizes the Church. The Church is not really Christ, but without the Church Christ cannot be met in his fulness — as the woman would not have met Jesus if she had not gone to the well. The Church is the sacrament of the encounter with Christ.

In evangelization, the Church plays a paramount role. First, because it is the "place" where the Spirit of Jesus is offered to us with the greatest intensity, where the gift of God and Christian experience are given with more power, where Jesus decisively acts to evangelize people.

It is true that Jesus through his Spirit acts everywhere and in all peoples, even those outside the Church. But it is in the Church that he acts in all his plenitude and riches. The Church is the "country" of Jesus, of the Holy Spirit, and of the experience of Christian faith.

To say Church is to speak of the gospel that is taught there, of its sacramentality, of its different community experiences, of its diverse ministries. In fact, Christian experience is eminently an experience of Church. Historically, to evangelize is to bring people to an experience of Church. We become Christians and we follow Jesus in the Church.